549

W9-DAG-558

BALBOA
Finder of the Pacific

BALBOA

FINDER OF THE PACIFIC

DISCARD

By RONALD SYME

Illustrated by WILLIAM STOBBS

WILLIAM MORROW AND COMPANY

New York   *1956*

7/78 WLS 521

JB
B

38539

Hiram Halle Memorial Library
Pound Ridge, New York
10576

© 1956 by William Morrow and Company, Inc. All rights reserved.
Published simultaneously in the Dominion of Canada by George J.
McLeod Limited, Toronto. Printed in the United States of America.
Library of Congress Catalog Card Number: 56-5181

15   75

Also by Ronald Syme

HENRY HUDSON
JOHN SMITH OF VIRGINIA
MAGELLAN, FIRST AROUND THE WORLD
LA SALLE OF THE MISSISSIPPI
COLUMBUS, FINDER OF THE NEW WORLD
CHAMPLAIN OF THE ST. LAWRENCE
CORTES OF MEXICO

All illustrated by William Stobbs

BAY OF THE NORTH

Illustrated by Ralph Ray

Seventeen-year-old Vasco Balboa was in a great hurry. He strode in through the big stone doorway and across the drafty hall, where dogs lay asleep under a long oak table.

His father was sitting in a heavy chair beside the fireplace. He looked up at the sound of Vasco's quick footsteps.

"Good day to you, my son," he said. "What has

caused you to ride twenty miles from the town and arrive here so early in the morning?"

"It is the news about the discovery made by Columbus, sire," Vasco replied. "Everyone in Spain is talking about it. People are saying there must be vast countries on the other side of the Atlantic. Captain Columbus himself believes it. He is already planning to make a second voyage. Other navigators are sure to follow him. Sire, I wish to join a ship sailing to this New World across the ocean."

Vasco's father looked at him thoughtfully. "You were not born with that red hair for nothing. You have a quick mind and a taste for reckless adventure. I thought this amazing discovery of Columbus might start you a-dreaming."

"You will let me go?" asked Vasco eagerly.

His father shook his head.

"No. Listen to me, Vasco. Our family name of Balboa is famous throughout Spain. For three hundred years we have been loyal soldiers of the king. Now you are being trained as the future head of our family. That is why you are a page in the palace of Don Pedro, the governor of this province. You are learning many useful things there." He ignored Vasco's impatience and continued evenly. "Already you have learned to read and write unusually well. This knowledge will be of great value to you in later life. What good would it be to give up your education now and go sailing across the ocean?"

"The Captain says there is gold in these new countries," Vasco persisted.

His father smiled.

"The Balboa family could use plenty of that, for we never have been wealthy. I've an idea, however, that all the gold of this New World won't be found within the next few years. Wait until you are older, my son. True, you are taller than most men, even now, but seventeen is early to start off on great adventures."

Vasco hesitated. He glanced at his father's lean and bearded face. There was an unusually firm expression on it.

"Very well, sire," said Vasco. "I will wait."

He waited dutifully for eight years. During that time, Columbus gradually located the islands of the Caribbean Sea, and the first Spanish settlers reached the fertile island of Hispaniola (Haiti). But Vasco, who was a sharp young man, noticed that not much gold was being found in the New World. Everyone still talked about it, and a certain number of gold ornaments were brought back to Spain, but no one had yet discovered where the raw metal came from. The explorers were kept too busy trying to make their way safely along mysterious coasts in clumsy little ships which carried no charts.

Then Vasco heard that one or two ships had brought back rich cargoes of pearls. Their captains had given the name *Pearl Coast* to the almost unknown northwestern shore of South America. Once again the taverns, the quays, and the drawing rooms were filled with excited talk about the fabulous riches of the New World. Aside from Columbus and a few other wise thinkers, no one spent much time wondering about what lay beyond the Pearl Coast and the Isthmus of Panama. Few of them dreamed that a whole undiscovered ocean was there, awaiting the first explorer.

Vasco Balboa was twenty-five years old when his chance to join an expedition to the New World finally came. A friend told him that a man named Bastidas had chartered two tiny ships for a voyage to the Pearl Coast. Bastidas hoped to buy enough pearls from the natives to make a fortune. Balboa went to see him.

"Sir," he said, "I would like to join your expedition. I have little money to pay for my passage, but perhaps I could be useful to you in other ways."

Bastidas looked at the tall young man with the bright red hair and manly face. He recognized the family name of Balboa. "Good swordsmen are always useful," he said. "I will arrange a passage for you."

Balboa left Spain in the year 1500. The two vessels were piloted by Juan de la Cosa, the skillful navigator who had sailed with Columbus on his second voyage. They made an easy crossing to the Pearl Coast, which later became Colombia.

Balboa leaned over the side of the ship and gazed wonderingly at thatched huts and palm trees on the nearby shore. Canoes darted out to meet the slowly moving ships. They were paddled by copper-skinned natives with straight black hair which reached to their shoulders. Some of them wore wreaths of flowers round their necks. As the canoes neared the vessels, the Indians held up coconut shells filled with glimmering pearls. They eagerly exchanged these pearls for needles, mirrors, knives, and lengths of cloth.

The natives along other parts of the coast were not so friendly. There the tribesmen were surly, bony-faced fellows who went naked and carried

bows and quivers of poisoned arrows. Cosa, the pilot, remembered these dangerous tribes. When he recognized them he kept the ships away from their shores. He and Balboa had become friends. Cosa gave the eager young man advice that was very useful to him later.

"East of yonder mountain live friendly tribes," he said. "West of it lives a dangerous one." Or again: "That wide stretch of white beach with the tall black rocks is unsafe for us. When I came with Columbus, we were attacked there."

Balboa remembered everything Cosa told him. He was fascinated by the bright green of the jungle, by glimpses of blue mountain peaks, and most of all by the splendid, glistening pearls. I'll come back here one day, he thought. A man could spend his whole life exploring the countries that must lie far inland.

Under Cosa's guidance, the two ships toiled westward until they reached a wide and deep fresh-water bay which was later named the Gulf of Urabá. Now the vessels began to swing northward along the coast of what is now Panama. Bastidas smiled and rubbed his hands with delight. The voyage had been wonderfully profitable. Down in the holds of his ships was a fortune in pearls.

Then suddenly there came disaster! Water began streaming into the vessels through innumerable tiny holes. Sea worms had drilled their way through the timbers. The hulls of the ships were so riddled with holes that they were little more than sieves.

Cosa hurriedly set course for Hispaniola. By pumping water day and night, the seamen managed to keep afloat while they fled northward across the Caribbean Sea. Just as they reached the western end of Hispaniola, both vessels sank in shallow water. Balboa and his friends waded ashore, lugging sacks full of pearls.

They were two hundred miles from the little town of Santo Domingo, the only Spanish settlement on the whole island. To reach it, they had to walk along hot, steaming jungle paths and over steep-sided mountains. The seamen had no food with them, so they exchanged mirrors, beads, and nails with the natives for corn, green vegetables,

and meat. The journey took two weeks, but at last
they reached Santo Domingo.

There, however, they found their troubles were
not yet ended.

The governor of Hispaniola arrested Bastidas and
his men and flung them into jail. He charged them
with having no license to trade with the natives. He

would not listen to their excuse that they had done so only to get food. Bastidas was sent to Spain as a prisoner, to be tried in a Spanish court. Balboa and the rest of the men were left in Hispaniola. The disagreeable governor also sailed for Spain, but his ship went down during an Atlantic gale and he was drowned. Bastidas was pardoned in Spain, sold his pearls, and made a nice fortune for himself. Meanwhile, the unlucky Balboa was left wondering how he was going to live in Hispaniola.

"You could buy land and slaves," his new friends told him, "but nowadays they cost a great deal of money. There is nothing for you in Hispaniola, Vasco. The island is already full of young men of good family who have no work and no money. Many of them are going hungry. It would be wiser for you to go back to Spain."

"Go back to Spain?" Balboa repeated. "No, my friends, I stay here. I have a few pearls to sell. When they are gone, I shall see what luck brings me. Surely there is enough land beyond this sea for any man able to go and find it."

Balboa stayed in Hispaniola eight years. During that time, few new discoveries were made around the shores of the Caribbean Sea. Men were too busy scheming to get land for themselves in newly settled Cuba and Jamaica. They still talked about going in search of new countries and an unknown ocean, but they did little about it.

Then, in 1509, a silly but brave young nobleman named Alonso de Ojeda was chosen by King Ferdinand of Spain to start a colony on the Pearl Coast. His territory lay several hundred miles east of a line drawn northward through the Gulf of Urabá. Ojeda sailed for the Pearl Coast with four ships and three hundred men. The famous pilot, Juan de la Cosa, went with him.

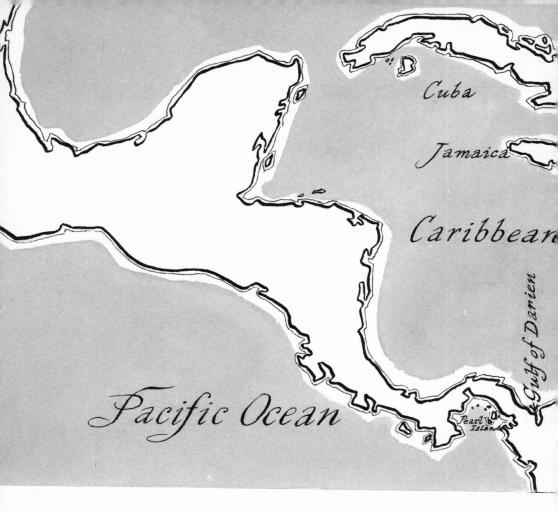

In Hispaniola, Vasco Balboa heard some interesting news.

"The lawyer, Martin Enciso," he was told, "is getting together a couple of ships to follow Ojeda

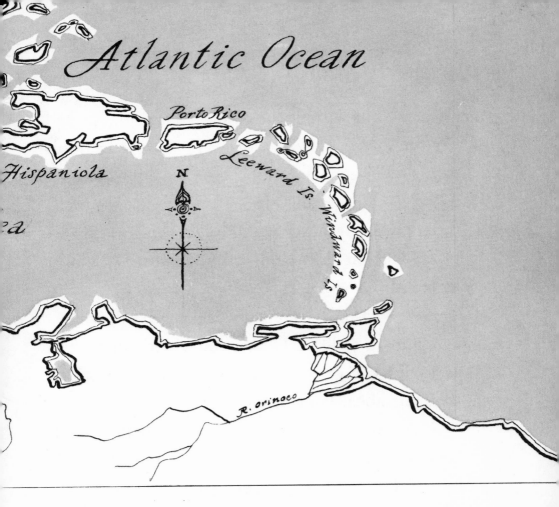

with more men and supplies of food. Enciso de-
clares he is going to be mayor of the new colony.
He and Ojeda reckon they will make a fortune out
of pearls."

Balboa said nothing, but his quick brain was already thinking out the details of a plan. He had been unlucky in Hispaniola. The money from his pearls had been spent long ago and he had many debts. If I miss this chance to go exploring, he thought, I may never get another. All the expeditions sail from Spain; none from Hispaniola. I must leave with Enciso.

There was only one drawback: Enciso, a conceited man, disliked Balboa and looked upon him as a wild young fellow. He would never agree to have him aboard one of his ships.

When the vessels were ready to sail, Balboa took his sword and his cloak. With his powerful bloodhound, Leoncico, he sneaked aboard Enciso's own ship in the middle of the night. He hid the big dog among a pile of sacks. He himself climbed into a large barrel and replaced the cover above his head.

The two vessels sailed at dawn. When they were

far out to sea, Balboa climbed out of his barrel, re-
leased the patient Leoncico, and strolled along the
deck to meet Enciso.

"I regret, sir," he said, "that I found myself
tempted to stow away aboard your ship."

Enciso almost choked with rage. At first he decided to dump Balboa ashore on the first land they
came to and leave him to look after himself. Two
thoughts stopped him. First, the men on the ships
liked this plucky young man with the sword and
the dog. They would probably mutiny if Balboa
were left to starve somewhere along the coast. Enciso also knew that Balboa had already been to the
Pearl Coast; his experience might be useful. He
grudgingly allowed Balboa to remain aboard his
ship.

The two ships sailed steadily onward. They were
nearing the Pearl Coast when they sighted a small
vessel hurrying northward toward them. It was

coming from Ojeda's new settlement. Aboard it were thirty-five haggard men.

"We are all that are left out of three hundred," the hollow-cheeked and starving passengers told Enciso. "Ojeda left us a month ago to seek help in Hispaniola. He has not returned. The Indians attacked us by day and night. We dared not plant gardens near the little fort we built, or go in search of food supplies. The savages were always waiting for us in the jungle with poisoned arrows. Had we stayed in San Sebastian—Ojeda's name for our settlement—we should all have died."

It was a terrible disappointment to Enciso. He refused to believe the story.

"You were cowards and ran away," he said accusingly. "Now I shall lead you back to San Sebastian and show you how to deal with a few troublesome natives."

Balboa shrugged his shoulders and walked away.

He knew about those wicked reedlike arrows. He also knew it was useless to warn the haughty Enciso. Presently he spoke to one of the survivors, who was hungrily devouring a plate of food.

"Friend, what happened to the pilot, Juan de la Cosa? Ten years ago we sailed together along the Pearl Coast. We were friends. He knew the natives well."

"Ojeda would not listen to Cosa's good advice about where to land," said the settler. "The young fool went ashore on a part of the coast where Cosa said the natives were lying in wait for us. Cosa went with him, even though he knew it meant almost certain death. Ojeda escaped when the savages attacked us. Cosa and many of our friends died." Then the man glanced round cautiously and added, "But we found some gold while we were cruising along the coast. Near the Gulf of Urabá there are tribes who wear many gold ornaments. All of us who still live have some of them hidden away."

When the three ships reached the settlement Ojeda had built, the voyagers saw that nothing was left of it except fire-blackened wooden walls and burned huts. The savages had destroyed the abandoned fort.

Enciso stared at the scene from the deck of his ship and began to fret. Was it possible that the survivors' story was true? He hastened to land, but his ship smashed onto a rock as they sailed into the bay.

It sank within ten minutes. There was no time to
save the horses and pigs, cannon, food, and gun-
powder aboard the ship.

Balboa and the crew stripped off their clothes
and swam ashore. They lost everything they owned,

except the dog Leoncico, who followed his master.
The other little vessels dropped anchor safely.

The hungry and frightened men began hastily
rebuilding the fort. Twenty of them were killed by
poisoned arrows in the first week.

Enciso had lost much of his money when the ship sank. Now it seemed likely he was going to lose his life. He had courage, but he was selfish and a bully. The scared men began to hate him as they cowered behind the wooden walls and hungrily chewed grass and roots. They saw that Balboa was the only cunning Indian fighter among them. He alone seemed to know what to do when the savages attacked. The men knew that, if they stayed on in San Sebastian, they were certain to die of starvation or be killed by those whispering, deadly arrows. They went to Balboa for advice.

"On the western side of this Gulf of Urabá," said Balboa, "there is a fair country. It is inhabited by warlike people, but at least they do not use poisoned arrows. Their villages are surrounded by gardens in which they grow many different kinds of fruit and vegetables. I think if I were your leader, I would take you there."

One of the men, burly, black-bearded Francisco Pizarro, grinned wickedly.

"If Enciso does not take us there," he said, "you *will* be our leader."

Enciso was glad enough to agree. He appointed Balboa as guide. In the two ships that remained, the starving and worn-out men fled from death in San Sebastian.

A day later the Spaniards gazed at a fertile valley running inland between hills that rose gradually to become mountain peaks. Leaf-thatched huts, surrounded by neat gardens, stood within a couple of hundred yards of the shore. There were also swamps and stagnant pools, but to the desperate men aboard the ships the cultivated land meant only one thing— food. They stormed ashore to slash with their swords at the six hundred warriors who were waiting for them.

The wooden swords and spears wielded by the

Indians were no match for steel weapons and armor. The natives fought with splendid bravery until half their force lay dead. Then they fled with their chief, Cémaco, to the safety of the jungle-covered hillsides. The starving Spaniards dashed to the huts, looking for food.

There was plenty of food in those huts. There was also gold. As the Spaniards gnawed cassava bread and mushrooms, they grabbed necklaces, bangles, and anklets. Afterwards they rested for three days, stirring only to find more food for themselves.

Enciso quickly recovered his nerve. His greedy nature made him think only of the gold the men had seized. He ordered them to hand it over to him.

"I am second in command to Ojeda," he said. "I will take care of the gold until he returns."

Neither Enciso nor his men knew it then, but Ojeda would never return. He had been ship-wrecked in Cuba, and had nearly died of hunger. When he finally reached Hispaniola, he was broken in health and spirit. He died a lonely death on that island.

The men muttered sulkily that they were deter-mined not to give up their gold. They chose Balboa to answer Enciso.

"Sir," Balboa said politely to the lawyer, "Ojeda's

territory lies *east* of a line drawn northward through the middle of the Gulf of Urabá. When we came here, we crossed that line. We are now to the *west* of it. This territory has been given by King Ferdinand to a young nobleman named Diego de Nicuesa. Neither you nor Ojeda has any authority at all in this new settlement of ours."

Enciso almost exploded with rage. He knew Balboa was right, but that did not improve his temper. He spoke violently of traitors and treachery. He threatened death by hanging to anyone who defied him. The tough band of seamen and adventurers turned on him.

"You are no longer our leader," they said. "Balboa is the man who saved all our lives, including your own, by bringing us here. He will be our captain until the rightful owner, Nicuesa, comes to claim this territory."

From that moment, Enciso became Balboa's

most deadly enemy. He never forgave him and worked without ceasing to ruin him.

Balboa immediately began putting the new settlement in order. He named it Darien, and appointed a sturdy young fellow named Martin Zamudio as alcalde, or mayor. He made friends with the defeated Indian tribe and gave them presents that delighted them. Only their chief, Cémaco, refused to meet Balboa. He remained hidden in the forest, seeking a way to avenge himself on the white-skinned invaders.

There was sufficient food at hand to keep the men fairly well fed, but Balboa encouraged them to plant crops of their own. He could do nothing, however, about the great vampire bats which bit men at night, the deadly mosquitoes, and the horrible toads which infested the huts. These were things which the settlers had to accept. They protected themselves against them as best they could.

Gold poured into Darien. The natives brought presents of it almost every day. They departed with axes and knives, which they valued much more. Before long, every man in Darien was richer than he had ever been before.

"Equal shares for everybody," said Balboa. "I'll make trouble for any man who tries to take too much."

At the same time, Balboa never forgot that this land legally belonged to the nobleman, Diego de Nicuesa. When a young sea captain named Colmenares came sailing in to Darien in search of Nicuesa, Balboa went quickly to see him.

"I have heard that Nicuesa set off from Hispaniola to explore the coast somewhere far west of here," Balboa told the captain. "You are his second in command, Colmenares. Go and find Nicuesa. Tell him that I have settled on his land, but that I am ready to turn it over to him whenever he arrives."

Colmenares sailed away, impressed with Balboa's honesty. He found young Nicuesa camping miserably on the coast not far from the Chágres River. The silly young man, who knew nothing about exploring or navigation, had run into great trouble. He had sailed from Hispaniola with five big ships and nearly eight hundred men. Now he was left with a dinghy and sixty starving followers. Hostile Indians, hunger, fever, and bad navigation had wiped out the rest.

Even now the young man had not learned sense. He rubbed his hands greedily when Colmenares told him about Balboa.

"How dare he and his fellows land on my territory!" he exclaimed angrily. "I'll order them to leave at once. What's more, I'll seize their gold. A dangerous rogue, this fellow Balboa! It's clear that he's led a mutiny against the lawyer, Enciso."

Two of Balboa's men had come with Captain Colmenares. They listened to the boastful Nicuesa's threats.

"He'll never be a leader like Balboa," they muttered to one another. "We'd better give our comrades warning of what this young fool intends to do when he gets to Darien."

They returned to Darien in one of the ship's boats and told the hard-faced settlers about Nicuesa's plans for them.

"We nearly died before we got here," grumbled Balboa's men. "We fought for what we have now. We built this settlement ourselves and freely elected Balboa as our leader. Are we going to be ordered round by a strutting young cockerel like Nicuesa?"

When the ship bringing Nicuesa reached Darien,

Balboa stood on the beach, at the head of his armed men.

"The settlers have voted against you, *Señor* Nicuesa," he called. "We are loyal to our king and country. We believe that this colony will be lost to Spain if you take it over. We intend to hold it. I am sorry that I have been chosen to tell you this, *Señor* Nicuesa," Balboa continued. "Go elsewhere and build a settlement of your own. We shall welcome any of your men who wish to remain with us. They are free to choose."

Nicuesa raged and pleaded. He threatened and nearly wept. His temper grew even worse when he saw Captain Colmenares and forty-eight of his men go ashore. They had looked at burly young Balboa and decided he was the better leader for them.

Nicuesa finally sailed away with seventeen men. None of them were ever heard of again. Somewhere or other they lost their lives and their ship. The

45

colony established by thirty-six-year-old Balboa and his small band in 1511 was the first successful European settlement on the American mainland.

The little settlement at Darien prospered, but it was too small to content Balboa. The distant mountains stirred his imagination. Day and night he wondered what lay beyond them. Eagerly he sought information from a chieftain named Careta, with whom he had made friends.

"I have heard that a great ocean lies far to the west," said Careta. "None of us have seen it, but perhaps the story is true. I do not know."

Nevertheless, during his first year in Darien, Balboa had little chance to go exploring. One by one, he defeated the Indian tribes who lived inland or along the coast. Time after time, his little band of soldiers fought against many hundred warriors armed with spears and bows. The Spaniards always won. Their armor was rusty and their weapons blunt, but their shields and their swords brought them victory. Cémaco, the Darien chieftain who had become their first enemy, was the one man they could never defeat. He lay in ambush for them in the forests or attacked small parties of soldiers. Whenever Balboa tried to entrap him, Cémaco always managed to slip away.

Balboa fell in love with the young and pretty daughter of Careta, the friendly chieftain, and married her. Her name has been forgotten, but not the part she played in Balboa's life, for she became his faithful and trusted adviser. She was wise enough to realize that it was better for all the tribes to make allies of the unbeatable Spaniards. On several occasions she brought Balboa and some Indian chief together in order to make peace.

A year after he had arrived in Darien, Balboa marched inland to fight a powerful chieftain named Comogre. Once again the Spaniards won. As usual, Balboa made friends with the defeated tribe.

"Why should we be enemies?" he asked Comogre. "Surely this country is large enough for all men to live peacefully in it. Let us be friends from now on. I have too few men to go on fighting all you great chieftains."

They shook hands. Comogre gave Balboa four

thousand ounces of gold as a present. The two leaders stood side by side to watch the Spanish craftsmen weigh and melt the gold. One of Comogre's seven sons stepped forward and pointed scornfully at the weighing machine.

"Why bother about so little gold? Beyond those mountain peaks there lies a great sea. Where the hills slope down to the beach, there is much gold to be found. All that territory belongs to King Tuba-namá. He is the richest chieftain in this whole land. Find a thousand soldiers, O Balboa, and I will lead you to the ocean. But remember that Tubanamá, my father's enemy, will try to destroy you."

Balboa marched back to Darien. He sent for Colmenares, the young ship's captain who had deserted Nicuesa.

"At last I have some real news about the ocean we call the Southern Sea," he said. "It is said to lie on the far side of these mountains. With so few men I dare not go in search of it. We need fresh volunteers and new weapons. I am willing to sail to Hispaniola to get these supplies, but many of the settlers are afraid to let me leave. They think some fresh trouble may arise while I am absent." Balboa smiled as he looked at Colmenares. "You have already gone to Hispaniola once on my behalf. Now I am asking you to go for me again."

Colmenares agreed to do this, and Balboa went on with his plans. "At the same time, I will send Enciso, the lawyer, back to Spain. As long as he stays in Darien he will go on trying to cause trouble. Martin Zamudio, our mayor, will go with him. Enciso will lie about what we have done in Darien, but Zamudio will tell the truth." Balboa paused a moment. He chuckled. "But that will be only one man's word against another's," he added. "The King will not know whom to believe. Colmenares, my friend, you, too, must go to Spain when you have finished our business in Hispaniola. Thus I will have two friends in the royal palace. You and Zamudio will take your share of gold with you when you go. We shall send you further shares from time to time."

Colmenares sailed for Hispaniola. His ship carried an enormous treasure. The faithful Balboa was sending King Ferdinand one fifth of all the gold

the men of Darien had obtained. It was the usual
arrangement in those days.

The new governor of Hispaniola sent three ships
and a hundred and fifty men to Darien. He also
forwarded a letter from the King, to whom Balboa
had written several months before. The letter made
Balboa the temporary governor of the whole province of Darien.

Holding the letter in his hand, Balboa watched

the sturdy new recruits coming ashore from the ships. There are not a thousand of them, he thought, but I can wait no longer before going in search of the Southern Sea. If Darien grows more wealthy, the King is sure to send a more important man than myself to be the governor here.

Balboa sat down and wrote a long letter to the King. After thanking him for the appointment, he said: "Since we came to Darien, I have had two thoughts constantly in my mind. One is to explore and develop fresh territories for Spain. The other is to care for my men, so that none shall lose their lives through any fault of mine."

When the ships returned to Hispaniola, the letter went with them.

Balboa mustered his men and selected one hundred and ninety of them. The new recruits were left behind in Darien. The men Balboa chose to cross the mountain ranges and fight their way to the

Southern Sea were hard-bitten fellows, accustomed to danger, hardship, and sickness.

"I have been told that a thousand fighting men are necessary for our journey," Balboa said to them. "There are nearly two hundred of us. If every man fights with the strength and courage of five, we shall reach our destination. Perhaps our rewards will be greater than any we have yet received. Come, let us start."

The tiny army marched out of Darien. At their head walked Balboa, with his dog Leoncico stepping beside him. In the rear came a large number of Indians who would act as guides, porters, and bridge builders.

The date was September 1, 1513.

"The swamps gave us much trouble," wrote Balboa. "Many times we had to wade through deep and foul-smelling mud and stagnant water for three, four, and five miles at a time. We placed our cloth-

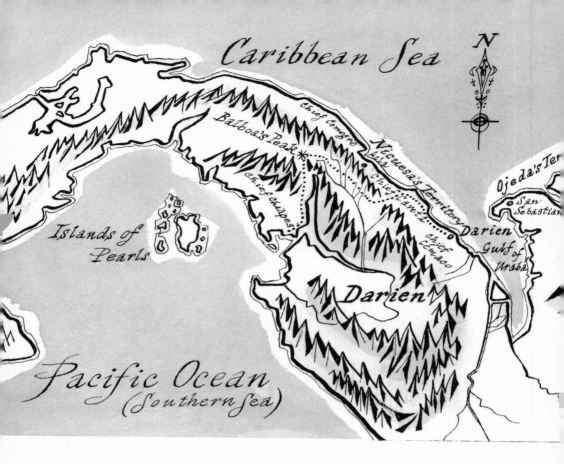

ing on top of our heads. No sooner were we free of one swamp than we came to another."

At last the hot and steaming lowlands were left behind. Now the marching men entered a silent, rain-wet forest. The tropical vegetation above their heads was so thick that it formed a canopy through which it was impossible to see the sky. Clad in armor and burdened with heavy weapons, the Spaniards began climbing the tremendous mountain barrier.

Whenever they came to a tiny village, Balboa made friends with the people. He realized it would be foolish to leave enemies between him and the coast of Darien. The Spaniards gave the natives axes and mirrors and knives. They received quantities of gold in return. "Gold is a soft and useless thing," said the Indians, "but with an ax a man can fell a tree."

Balboa left twelve sick men in the care of one chieftain, who supplied him with fresh guides. One hundred and seventy-nine Spaniards continued the agonizing march. Soon they were faced with vertical cliffs, down which cascaded roaring waterfalls. Sometimes they had to cross deep gorges on frail bridges made from forest creepers. Even for lightly

clad men, the journey would have been exhausting; for the armor-clad Spaniards it was a terrible nightmare.

Nevertheless, when a hostile chieftain named Quarequá charged at the head of a thousand warriors, Balboa's men stood shoulder to shoulder to meet the onslaught. When their muskets were empty, they fought with sword and ax and dagger. Leoncico, the bloodhound, took a ferocious and effective part in the fighting. Quarequá and six hundred of his warriors died that day. Not a single Spaniard was killed, and only a few were wounded.

Once again Balboa and his men struggled on up the mountains, to a region where the winds blew keenly and the nights were cold. Only seventy men followed him now. The rest had been left in various villages. Some were suffering from wounds, others from fever. A number had collapsed from the hardships of the dreadful journey.

On the morning of September 25, 1513, an Indian guide pointed to a nearby mountain peak.

"A man standing on its summit," he said, "can see the ocean."

Balboa set off to climb the hill, with Leoncico as his only companion. The journey took him two hours, for he was desperately tired. As he drew near the rocky summit, he realized that he might be approaching the greatest moment of his life. If nothing was visible except more mountains, then his first attempt to find the Southern Sea would have failed. The men were too exhausted to travel much farther without rest and proper food. But if the sea was visible, then he, Vasco Nuñez de Balboa, would be the man who had found it. He would be the first European to see the new ocean.

Balboa reached the summit. Eagerly he gazed westward. Far away in the distance lay the Pacific Ocean! Sunshine was sparkling on an expanse of blue water that matched the brightness of the morning sky.

Balboa raised his arm to salute the splendid sight. Now, whatever happened, his name would be remembered in centuries to come. He fell on his knees and began to pray. Far away at the bottom of the hill, seventy Spaniards looked at one another and grinned. They nodded their heads approvingly.

Once again their leader, redheaded Vasco Balboa, had led them to success.

"We have found our ocean," Balboa said to his companions. "Now I want to stand beside it."

The little band of men started down the western slope of the mountains. They were very tired by this time. The joints of their armor creaked rustily, and the damp heat of the forest was rotting the strings of their crossbows. Several Spaniards had to be helped along by native guides, and one or two were carried in hammocks.

One more Indian chief, a warrior named Chiapes, stood between Balboa and the sea. Once again the Spaniards stood shoulder to shoulder to face a fierce charge. They fired one volley from their clumsy muskets and then fought with swords. Chiapes' warriors fled, and the road to the sea lay open before them.

"Make friends with Chiapes and his men," said Balboa. "I want no enemies even now."

The surprised and grateful chieftain found himself being treated kindly by the Spaniards. He and Balboa became friends from the moment they met.

"Rest awhile in my village," said Chiapes. "You are great fighters, but I can see that you are also weary men."

Balboa agreed, even though he was impatient to reach the coast. He sent out a patrol led by a man named Alonso Martin to find the quickest path to the sea.

Two days later, Martin walked out of the forest and into hot sunshine. Bright wavelets were lapping the white beach, and frigate birds wheeled and hovered above the black rocks. A canoe lay on the sand. The men launched the little craft, and Alonso Martin climbed into it.

"Our leader found this ocean," he called to his

friends, "but I ask you to witness that I am the first European to float on its surface."

A few days later, Balboa himself stood on the beach. Holding the royal flag of Spain in one hand and his drawn sword in the other, he stepped into the warm sea until the water reached his knees. Solemnly, and in a loud voice, he claimed the Pacific Ocean and the whole American continent for his country.

"And these lands and seas," he ended, "shall belong to royal Spain so long as the world may last."

Balboa returned to the beach. He sat down in the shade with Leoncico beside him. For a long time he gazed across the bright surface of the Southern Sea, wondering what lay beyond its horizon. How many days' sail was it to the East Indies? How far to India, which the Portuguese were trying to reach by sailing round the southern tip of Africa? In which direction did China lie?

"We know from the great traveler, Marco Polo, that those countries really exist," he said thoughtfully. "I would give all my gold to be able to go with the men who will one day sail westward from these shores in search of them. I have opened the gate to this ocean, but perhaps others will be the first to pass through it."

Chiapes, Balboa's latest friend, had come with him to the shore. Now the chieftain raised his hand and pointed out to sea.

"There is a little island out there," he said, "which a canoe can reach in half a day. From there to the Pearl Islands, which lie much farther out to sea, our best pearls come."

It was a bad time of the year for voyaging. Squalls and storms were likely to blow up at any time. But Balboa was determined to see the nearest little island for himself.

"We have explored by land," he said to his grinning companions. "Now we will go exploring by sea. Up to the present, my voyages have not been very successful!"

Sixty Spaniards crowded into nine large canoes carved out of tree trunks and manned by Indian crews of paddlers. Four miles out to sea, a fierce wind arose, bringing with it a violent rainstorm. The canoes lurched and staggered across the waves. With water swirling round their feet, the Spaniards started to pray. They stripped off their armor so they could swim if necessary. Finally the canoes reached shelter beside a tiny islet.

The islet was no more than a few rocks projecting above the sea, but the Spaniards and Indians climbed ashore. They stood on this speck of land all night, while the sea rose and waves washed as high as their waists. When morning came, all the canoes were badly damaged.

"If they will carry us back to the mainland," said

Balboa, "we shall have a lot to be thankful for. Our supplies of food have gone and so has our drinking water."

The Indians managed to patch the broken canoes well enough to float them. The whole party paddled hastily back to the coast.

No sooner had the Spaniards stepped ashore, wet and tired, hungry and thirsty, than they were attacked by the warriors of another tribe. Once again Balboa and his men fought savagely and bitterly. When the Indians fled, Balboa sent a messenger to find their chief, Tumaco.

"You attacked us without reason while we were starving and exhausted," he said. "Nevertheless, I bear you no ill will. Give me your hand in friendship."

Tumaco accepted Balboa's offer. He gave some interesting news to the Spaniards.

"Far, far south of here," he said, "a great and

powerful nation lives on the coast. They have large canoes which are moved by sails, and the people carry their burdens on the backs of strange animals."

Tumaco drew a rough sketch of a llama in a patch of wet ground. The Spaniards stared at it wonderingly. Among them was burly Francisco Pizarro. He remembered Tumaco's words. A few years later, he sailed southward to discover the Inca nation of Peru.

Loaded with pearls and an immense fortune in gold, Balboa and his men began their long march home to Darien. The chieftains with whom they had made friends wept as they said good-by.

"When you came to our villages we hated and feared you," they said. "Now, by your kindness, you have become our good friend. Visit us again as soon as you can. We will sail together to the Islands of Pearls, and your men shall be guests in our villages."

"I will come back if I can," said Balboa, smiling. "Next time, however, I will travel in something larger than a canoe."

The journey back to Darien was even worse than the outward one. Balboa chose a new route in order to see more of this vast country. He knew that the route lay through the territory of Tubanamá, the greatest and most warlike chieftain, but it made no difference to him. The dry season had come, and in several regions the men nearly died of thirst. Then came a savage battle against Tubanamá, which lasted two hours and left the Spaniards victorious, but utterly exhausted.

Balboa himself collapsed from fever, exhaustion, and loss of blood from his wounds. He rested four days, then led his men down the mountain slopes to the sea and the shelter of Darien.

"We have found the Southern Sea," he told the colonists who had been left behind, "and we have also found much treasure. Unluckily, our health is not as good as the gold and pearls we bring you now."

Balboa had been absent from Darien for five months. In spite of four battles, long marches through fever-haunted forests, and lack of proper rations, he had not lost the life of a single man.

When the King of Spain received Balboa's letter

about his discovery of the Southern Sea, he was delighted. He wrote back to Darien at once. Balboa was awarded the title of Admiral of the Pacific and given various special powers. The King also ordered several ships to prepare to sail to Darien with all kinds of stores. One of these vessels was to carry the King's secret envoy, a decent and straight-spoken man named Arbolancha.

"Go to Darien and find out what Balboa is really doing," King Ferdinand said to him. "Do not let him know why you have come. Bring me back a true report on him. I think he is a brave soldier and a great explorer, but I wish to be sure."

The ships were prepared for the voyage. Happily the King began to count the enormous treasure of gold and pearls that Balboa had sent him. Its size had set all Spain talking.

Balboa was a popular hero, but there were men who hated him. Enciso, the lawyer, was still in Spain. Like the sea worm that ruins timber, he worked patiently and secretly, trying to ruin Balboa.

"The redheaded ruffian stole the territory belonging to Ojeda and me," he said. "He drove me out when I protested. Now he is trying to build an independent kingdom for himself in Darien. It is true that he is sending some gold to Spain, but he is certainly keeping more than his rightful share of it. Balboa is a cunning villain who has fooled our good King."

There were no proper maps of the Pearl Coast. No one in Spain knew where Darien was. They did not know that it lay west of the boundary line through the Gulf of Urabá, so they did not realize that Enciso had absolutely no claim at all to Darien. That territory belonged rightfully to Nicuesa, but Nicuesa was lost and dead.

Enciso carefully avoided telling anyone that Ojeda had been driven out of his own territory by the Indians. Nor did he mention that Balboa had saved the lives of the whole party by guiding them to the new settlement at Darien. Day and night, Enciso whispered and lied, complained and plotted. He was as clever as a fox and finally managed to turn many of the highest officials at the royal palace against Colmenares and Zamudio, the two trust-

worthy men whom Balboa had sent home from Darien to represent him in Spain. They were in danger of being murdered by Enciso's secret agents and had to go into hiding.

The King heard Enciso's lying stories and decided it might be wiser to appoint a new governor in Darien. Balboa would then be left free to carry on his great work of exploration. The person chosen as governor was an evil man named Pedrarias Dávila.

Dávila was intensely jealous of anyone more successful than himself. He was a good soldier, but he
was also narrow-minded, cruel, and greedy. From
the moment he was appointed, Dávila made up his
mind to get rid of Balboa. True, the King had hon-
ored Balboa, but Dávila knew it would be easy to
frame false charges against him somehow or other.

The enormous treasure which had arrived from

Darien made people in Spain think that Darien was a great and growing city. The little settlement of thatched huts had foolishly been given the misleading name of Castilla del Oro (Golden Castile). Hundreds of rich young men struggled and schemed to sail with Pedrarias Dávila. They believed they would be able to pick up gold on the hillsides, pearls on the shore. None of them realized the hardships and poor conditions that really existed in Darien. Dávila and his glittering fleet of ships sailed in April, 1514.

Arbolancha, the King's secret agent, was already in Darien. He quickly saw how the colonists liked and respected Balboa. He watched while their leader carefully weighed and divided all gold and pearls, always putting aside the one fifth that belonged to the King. Arbolancha also noted that Balboa ate the same food as his men and lived in a hut that was little better than anyone else's. He wore plain clothes, watched carefully over his men's welfare, and was friendly with all the chieftains of the territory. Enciso has been lying, thought Arbolancha. This Balboa is no rebel. Spain could do with a hundred like him. He is a good and faithful officer of King Ferdinand.

Arbolancha hastened to prepare the ships for their homeward voyage. He had news now that the King should know quickly. He already knew what Enciso and his friends were plotting in Spain. Now he knew that everything they said was a lie. But by the time Arbolancha reached Spain, Pedrarias Dávila had already sailed. It was too late to save Balboa.

When Dávila's ships arrived at Darien, a thousand fashionable young men hung over the ship's side and stared in horror at Golden Castile. Was this huddle of thatched cottages, situated on dusty, sun-dried ground, the rich town they had believed

Darien to be? Were those poorly dressed men, with faces yellow from fever, the wealthy settlers of Castilla del Oro?

Their spirits sank even lower when Balboa invited all the new arrivals to a feast. The guests, who had been accustomed to white tablecloths and sparkling cutlery, found themselves eating off wooden plates with wooden forks and clumsy knives. Instead of roast joints and rich wines, they ate cassava bread and pineapples, and drank tepid water from the nearest stream.

The guests stared with wonder at Balboa himself. Was this burly young man in white shirt and knee breeches the conqueror of Darien, the finder of the Southern Sea? He spoke quietly and in a friendly manner to the slaves who brought the food. There was no trace of boasting in his voice. And yet, thought the young men enviously, this was the Balboa who had sent a vast fortune to Spain and who was a very wealthy man himself.

The young noblemen did not worry long. Fifty of them died of fever during the first week. Seven hundred were dead at the end of two months. Dávila, the governor, now hated Balboa as well as envying him. He spent his time waiting and watching for a chance to bring him to trial.

Balboa grew tired of the constant grumbling and

squabbling that had arisen in Darien. He longed to set off on another journey of exploration. He remembered the strange stories about a great empire somewhere far to the south. He had also heard that on the coast a hundred miles north of Darien there grew trees which were considered especially valuable for shipbuilding. Their timber was supposed to resist the attacks of marine borer worms.

"We'll cut down sufficient trees and take the logs across the mountains to the west coast," said Balboa. He was determined to sail south along the west coast of South America.

The giant task seemed impossible. It was one of the most extraordinary journeys ever attempted. Huge gangs of Indian workers with Spanish foremen hauled the great logs up cliffs and slung them across yawning ravines in whose depths, far below, rivers ran fast and furiously. Somehow the workers

managed to haul, push, and half carry the logs to the summit of the mountains. Then they dragged the timber down the western slopes to the Pacific Ocean, only to find that it was the worst they had ever tried to use. Borer worms drilled holes in the logs as soon as they were placed in the sea!

Balboa was undaunted. "We'll cut down trees on this coast," he said. "The ships must be built."

He watched eagerly while Spanish craftsmen made two small brigantines of not more than forty tons each.

"Now we'll go exploring again," Balboa said to his friends. "We'll sail to the Pearl Islands and use them as our base. From there we'll travel southward toward the strange country that Chief Tumaco described to us."

Balboa sent one of his men back to Darien to tell Dávila that he intended to set off on another voyage of exploration. The messenger chosen was

Andres Garabito, one of the settlers who had accompanied Balboa to Darien from San Sebastian, and had marched with him to the Southern Sea. Garabito was wildly jealous of Balboa, but he had always managed to hide his jealousy. Balboa trusted him entirely. The mistake was to cost him his life.

Garabito hastened to Darien. "Balboa is planning to sail southward to found a new kingdom for himself," he reported to Dávila. "He has two ships ready and another two building. Three hundred men are ready to go with him."

Pedrarias Dávila nodded his head coldly. Inwardly he must have been jubilant. Here was his chance. He could bring Balboa to trial for treason. As the all-powerful governor of this faraway province of Darien, it would be easy to force a conviction.

Dávila wrote a friendly letter to Balboa. He asked him to come to a little village named Acla, on the eastern coast, to discuss the plans for the voyage.

Balboa did not suspect a plot. As soon as he arrived in Acla, he entered the small house where he was to stay. Pizarro, the black-bearded soldier who had accompanied him to the Pacific, and several other armed men were waiting for him. They seized him quickly. Even then, Balboa did not realize what was happening.

"What are you doing, Francisco?" he said to Pizarro. "This is a strange kind of greeting."

Balboa was brought to secret trial by Dávila's orders. The charge against him was that he had built four ships in which to escape to the unknown country of Peru. The false charges made by Enciso were also brought up again. Of course Dávila knew by this time that Enciso had lied, but that made no difference to him.

Balboa now realized that Dávila was determined to put him to death.

"I have always served my king and my country faithfully," he said. "The voyage I planned was one that might have brought fresh glory and wealth to Spain."

His words unheeded, the forty-two-year-old explorer was sentenced to death. So eager was the evil Dávila to get rid of him that the execution took place at dawn the following day.

By the time the colonists in Darien heard the news, Balboa, finder of the Pacific Ocean and the New World's first shipbuilder, lay buried on the mountainside.

RONALD SYME spent his boyhood in New Zealand, sailing and hunting wild boar much of the time. At sixteen, he left school and went to sea in a Pacific cargo steamer, and for four years he traded between Australia, New Zealand, San Francisco, and the South Sea Islands. At eighteen, he began writing short stories, and in 1934 he left the sea to become a professional writer.

During World War II Mr. Syme served in the British Merchant Service as a gunner until he was transferred to the British Army Intelligence Corps because he spoke four foreign languages. He also fought with the Eighth Army in Africa and became a paratrooper during the Italian campaign.

Today Mr. Syme is a well-known author in both England and the United States. An insatiable voyager, he still continues to visit various portions of the globe, for research or pleasure. He recently sailed 1660 miles in a twenty-ton schooner from New Zealand to Rarotonga in the Cook Islands, where he now lives.

38539

J
B   BALBOA
SYME
   BALBOA

DISCARD

Myram Holls Memorial Library
Scaly Ridge, New York